# Carnival in New Orleans, a Fantasy

*Text and poems by*

Maurice Le Gardeur

*Illustrations by*

Robert Seago

*Music by*

John Preble

A Poetic Fantasy on Carnival & Mardi Gras
*Presenting the People, Politicians, and Problems in America's Playground*
*(With a Special Message to Texans and a Plea for Financial Assistance)*

<u>**WARNING:**</u>

This book may not be suitable for fundamentalist Christians
(Catholics can seek forgiveness on Ash Wednesday)
After purchase if you find anything in this book to be offensive,
You may either burn your copy or black it out with a Marks-A-Lot,
but under no circumstances can you get your money back!
However, if you burn your copy we'll just print more!

# Also by Maurice Le Gardeur

# Acknowledgements

In no particular order I would like to expressly thank the following for their substantial contributions to this work, which were causes in fact of its birth, and without whom it would not have hatched—at least not in its present iteration:

To the City of New Orleans, its people and politicians, who made the creation of this book a joy; to the well-read Mrs. Gloria Hopkins who convinced her son-in-law that my writing was worthy of his art; to John Preble who lives in a parallel universe of his own making which I am privileged to visit on occasion; to Andrew Preble, John's son, who bridged both worlds and finally brought this book kicking and screaming between the covers; to Glenda Hardey who gave me enough time to turn a second thought into a work of art; to Robert Seago whose Mardi Gras art inspired this book and made it beautiful; to Benita Kelly, my former secretary, who left me alone to my own devices; to Jacquie Rhodes, my new secretary, who danced through it all; to Richard Watts, Esq., who recognized raw talent when he thought he saw it; to the brilliant Marian Livaudais, Esq., who never stopped laughing; to Richard Grant who told me never to apologize; and finally to Arthur Hardy whose constructive criticism resulted in several re-writes and made this a much better book.

The Author

The Bard's Press
c/o Maurice Le Gardeur
222 N. Massachusetts St.
Covington, LA 70433
1-888-270-5177

www.bardofbostonstreet.com


©2009 Maurice Le Gardeur. All rights reserved.
ISBN: 978-0-9841222-1-9

Assembled by Andrew Preble
Original design by Glenda Hardey


Published by The Bard's Press, Covington, LA
Printed in China


Cover illustrations by Robert Seago


First edition


Copies of this book can be obtained from your bookseller,
or online at www.artcardsnola.com

Written for and dedicated
to our beloved visitors,
(especially Texans)
who love New Orleans
as much as we do.

*My, people come and go so quickly here.*
Dorothy from The Wizard of Oz

Blessed are they
who can laugh at the themselves
for they shall never cease
to be amused.

*An old Irish proverb*

# Contents

# Arthur's Comment[1]

Maurice Le Gardeur's irreverent wit combined with Robert Seago's elegant Mardi Gras art, make this Carnival collection lovely to look at and fun to read.

# Author's Comments

From Epigraph to Benediction a colorful Carnival ride through New Orleans ending in a Hurricane and Recovery—a brand New Addition to Mardi Gras Art, Mythology, and Music in the real-life Emerald City by natives who know it all!

Reader's Choice
*(hint: there are no wrong answers)*
( ) it's an art book
( ) it's a story book
( ) it's a joke book
( ) it's a poetry book
( ) it's a music book
( ) it's a gift book
( ) it's a history book
( ) it's a souvenir book
( ) it's a coffee-table book
( ) it's a cook book
( ) it's all of the above

Although a bit unconventional I created these comments. They are mostly true.[2] Since I wrote the book who knows more about it than I do?

---

1   Arthur Hardy, publisher, Mardi Gras Guide
2   As a lawyer or a poet I am licensed to stretch the truth- but as a lawyer-poet I am permitted to tear it apart! (If you want the Gospel and the whole story about Carnival and Mardi Gras see *Arthur Hardy's Mardi Gras in New Orleans, An Illustrated History*) See www.mardigrasguide.com to order his book.

# Introduction

## Ecoutez, S'il Vous Plait

What is Carnival in New Orleans, and particularly Mardi Gras, but a FANTASY—an annual occasion based on the alignment of the planets when a Prince can become a Pauper, a Pauper a Prince, and lots of guys in the Quarter Queens for a Day!

This book, like Carnival, is as unconventional as the subject matter it describes. Unlike a novel it has no beginning, middle, or end. Essentially it is a stream of consciousness centered around a poem which itself has no beginning, middle, or end, but memorializes an event which is central to the culture of New Orleans. It also includes the enchanting illustrations of native New Orleanian, Robert Seago, as well as the riotous songs of composer/songwriter and former *Chalmation*, John Preble, who produced the *New Mardi Gras Classics* compact disc provided inside the back cover pocket of this volume.

If you can't be here in New Orleans to enjoy your fantasy in person this book may help you create your own wherever you may be. Everything is here—comedy, satire, one-liners, poetry, art, history, music, and food (Creole recipes). All you have to supply is a costume and your favorite adult beverage. To paraphrase an old song:

> *Come along with me*
> *To the Mississippi*
> *We'll take a boat*
> *To the Land of Dreams*
> *Steam down the River*
> *Down to New Orleans!*

*Carnival in New Orleans, A Fantasy* is not written for our locals. If they want to read it or even buy it I won't stop them. It is written for and dedicated to our most desired visitors—our beloved tourists; or if you are from Texas or an Hispanic—*touristas*. New Orleans was

once full of Hispanics.  In the 18th century they were called Span-iards (between 1763 and 1800, Louisiana belonged to Spain).  So *bienvenidos!*  Why have you been gone so long?

As the author I would suggest that you read the book in the order presented.  For those readers who don't or won't follow suggestions (and you know who you are) you may want to read the glossary first and then whatever else pleases you.  (If you are an appellate judge you probably want to check out the footnotes first.)

As a New Orleanian I am the last person to tell anyone what to do because I don't like bossy people myself—just ask my parish priest, *Fr. Whatshisname, O.S.B.*[1]

# A Headnote[2]

The fun is in the footnotes so don't overlook them.  As a lawyer who has been writing legal briefs for nearly 40 years (including law school), I have learned to love footnotes.  They are the seasoning in the sauce!  In fact, I coined the term *toenote* (abbreviated T), which is a footnote to a footnote, and also *nailnote* (abbreviated N), which is a footnote to a toenote.  They are liberally sprinkled herein like  filé in gumbo.[3]  When you're spitting nailnotes you're really cooking!

I also love run-on sentences as they save on punctuation even though they may leave you breathless.

I also have a natural tendency to rhyme prose which I must fight every night I write—see what I mean.  I was born with the gift which surfaced during my first exposure to *Mother Goose*.  It was enhanced by my study of Wordsworth in high school and Frost in college and even spilled over into my French...

*C'est la vie, Cherie!*

---

1   This is not a construction material, but the *Order of St. Benedict.*
2   On the footnotes
3   Because you must have 20/20 vision (corrected) to read a toenote and a magnifying glass to read a nailnote, I have purposefully enlarged them for my contemporary readers who must put their glasses on during the day and take their teeth out at night.

# A Taste of New Orleans

Most people in this world eat to live—in New Orleans we live to eat, where every meal is viewed as a special occasion for family and friends to celebrate life and enjoy each other's company. There is no question that if you love good food you have come to the culinary capital of the world—the PURPLE, GREEN, and GOLD STANDARD against which all other eateries are measured. Even our neighborhood restaurants would rate 4 stars in any other city in the country and our home cooking is second to none with local signature dishes like red beans and rice, shrimp creole, gumbo, Bananas Foster, and even pralines. In addition to a dash of Tabasco in our main course we love a splash of brandy in our dessert and coffee.

New Orleans is also known as the birthplace of the COCKTAIL[4] which is discussed ad nauseam[5] in the Booze Section beginning on page 25.

Appendix III contains Creole recipes for six famous New Orleans dishes which are commonly served during the Carnival season. With these recipes you can prepare our fare in your kitchen whenever you can find our ingredients.[6]

Visit our website www.artcardsnola.com for other available recipes and local artwork by our illustrator Robert Seago.

---

4   This is not a poultry part.
5   This is an appropriate term in this context.
6   Good luck finding fresh crawfish in Amarillo—no you may not substitute scorpions.

# Preface

*An Introduction to Carnival Terminology and Interesting Facts about Mardi Gras Including a Brief History of New Orleans, America's Most Interesting City, with a Comprehensive Plan to Save the City, Restore our Coast, and Stimulate the Economy*

When you drive across the state line, which is in the middle of a bridge, you come to a sign which reads *Bienvenue la Louisiane.* Like Dorothy and her dog you know you aren't in Kansas anymore, or even Mississippi for that matter. And when you cross the bridge over Lake Ponchartrain you realize you aren't even in Louisiana anymore. You have arrived in New Orleans which is a real-life Emerald City.[1] New Orleans is known by more aliases than any other city in the world, among them: La Nouvelle Orleans, Isle d'Orleans, the Crescent City, the City that Care Forgot, the Big Easy, N'awlins, NOLA (an acronym for New Orleans, LA), the Home of the Saints, the Birthplace of Jazz, Hollywood South, Babylon on the Bayou, Bienville's Dilemma, Gateway to the Americas, Hurricane Alley, a Confederacy of Dunces, the Land of Dreams, Heaven on Earth, a Banana Republic, a Melting Pot, a Gumbo, an Artist Colony, a Musicians' Village, Café au Lait, and most recently Chocolate City. (If I missed a few forgive me because New Orleans is a work in progress.) How can one place have all these names? All these names are needed to describe a place which defies description. Because New Orleans is not merely a place, it is a state of mind limited only by the imagination of its people and its visitors. So how to describe an indescribable event, like Carnival, which is the heart and soul of an indescribable place? *Perhaps a poem.* But before we get to the poem, a brief introduction is helpful.

To our Mardi Gras visitors from other climes and countries (including Texas) some historical background, which native New Orleanians already possess, is needed for a full understanding of Carnival in New Orleans.

---

1   wwOZ is New Orleans' Jazz and Heritage radio station at 90.7 F.M. (Gentilly Boulevard should also be renamed the Yellow Brick Road.)

Mardi Gras is New Orleans' favorite holiday—like Christmas, New Year's Eve, the Fourth of July, and Halloween all rolled into one. Mardi Gras is French for Fat Tuesday—Mardi being the French word for Tuesday and Gras the French word for fat. The French have a bad habit of placing their adjectives behind the nouns they modify which comes out Tuesday Fat. You should never ever use the term Mardi Gras Day because you will show your ignorance and people may think you are from Texas. In effect you would be saying Fat Tuesday Day or Tuesday Fat Day, which is ignorant either way. If you want to say, Carnival Day, that's okay. Contrary to popular belief among Texans and other rednecks, Mardi Gras and Carnival are not the same thing. Mardi Gras is the last day of the Carnival season. Carnival begins on the twelfth night after Christmas and extends to Mardi Gras which is forty days, excluding Sundays, before Easter Sunday. Easter depends on the alignment of the planets, Easter being the first Sunday after the first full moon following the Spring Equinox. Mardi Gras is always the Tuesday before Ash Wednesday, the beginning of Lent.

The Mardi Gras tradition in New Orleans began in earnest when an elaborate parade[2] and party was thrown in honor of the Russian Grand Duke Alexis who visited New Orleans in 1872. The Grand Duke's favorite colors, purple, green, and gold became the official colors of the Carnival season, although LSU fans who bleed purple and gold and routinely beat the Tulane Green Wave in most sporting contests may argue the point.

Although New Orleans has the reputation of being a cosmopolitan city, in reality it is one of the most provincial places in the United States. Most New Orleanians have never even been to Texas and won't go near the place because they are afraid of being stepped on by a horse, cow, or buffalo, or of being attacked by Indians, or by the Mexican army on its way to reclaim the Alamo. In the second to last line of the poem, *And may I be damned to Texas* inferential reference is made to Texas as Hades, which lies beyond the River Styx, (in actuality the Sabine River), which is the boundary line separat-

---

2   This was the first Rex parade.

ing Louisiana and Texas. This reference reflects the love/hate[3] relationship New Orleanians have with Louisiana's larger, drier, richer, higher, oilier, and more obnoxious neighbor to the west. New Orleanians want Texans to visit New Orleans to spend money, but as soon as they're broke we want them to go home and take their silly hats and boots with them. Our Cajuns, who prefer rubber boots and who are often ridiculed as Coonasses by Texans, love to say *the only difference between a Coonass and a Jackass is the Sabine River.*

The final line in Carnival in New Orleans (*If ever I cease to love*) is a reference to the title and refrain from our famous Mardi Gras anthem of the same name which is included as Appendix I.

New Orleans is actually an island located between Lake Ponchartrain and the Mississippi River that will soon find itself in the middle of the Gulf of Mexico according to some global warming pundits, where it can seek independence and take its rightful place as a true banana republic instead of being a mere pretender. By then, Edwin Edwards[4] should be out on work release and be available for permanent appointment as New Orleans' resident wizard and casino host.

No one can deny that New Orleans is a city of survivors since it has survived the Spanish, the French, the British, the Pirates of the Caribbean (like Jean Lafitte who helped Andrew Jackson win the Battle of New Orleans which actually took place after the War of 1812 had ended), cholera and yellow fever epidemics, voodoo spells, floods, hurricanes, fires, slavery, the Civil War, Union blockades, Reconstruction, carpetbaggers, crooked politicians, prostitution (Storyville), Prohibition, the Great Depression, the Catholic Church, the Longs (both Huey and Earl), the Oil Companies, the U.S. Army Corps of Engineers, FEMA's Michael "Good-Job" Brown, President George W. Bush (a former Texas

---

3   After coaching The Green Wave for three seasons and taking Tulane to the Independence Bowl in 1987, Coach Mack Brown's tenure with Texas hasn't been any easier to stomach than Coach Nick Sabin's adultery with Alabama. These mortal sins, which even the Vatican can't indulge, make New Orleanians want to barf their beignets!

4   Former Louisiana governor Edwin Edwards could not be found guilty by a New Orleans jury- (he survived two attempts) and finally had to be tried in Baton Rouge before he could be convicted and sentenced to federal prison.

governor), and even New Orleans' peripatetic[5] and prophetic[6] Wizard/Mayor, C. Ray Nagin. The jury is still out on the nutria.[7]

Contrary to theories[8] preached by the scientific community (which is located north of Bunkie in Yankee cities like Chicargo and Noo Yawk), New Orleans is NOT threatened by global warming, rising sea levels, or subsidence due to the strangulation of nutrients from the Mississippi River by its levee system. Instead of creating new theories scientists should listen to our locals who know better. We know that the *one and only* threat to New Orleans' future existence is the *nutria*.[9] Everyone in New Orleans, and Southeast Louisiana for that

5   Ray is always out of town—often in Dallas, Texas.
6   *This city will be chocolate at the end of the day!* (Café au Lait wasn't good enough for Ray! Ray could pass for milk chocolate but he's also high in oxidants and free radicals—just ask the city council. Ray's shiny head could also pass for a #16 Brunswick bowling ball at Rock n' Bowl if he would shave off that shadow of a moustache.)
7   The nutria, *Myocastor coypus*, is a large semi-aquatic rodent. The generic name is derived from two Greek words (mys for mouse and kastor for beaver) that translate to mouse beaver.
8   Which includes *The Law of Gravity, The Theory of Relativity*, and other heretical apostasies like *Darwin's Theory of Evolution*[T1]
    [Toenote 1]  In response to this rampant secularism, Louisiana has recently passed SB 733 entitled *The Louisiana Science Education Act* which was unanimously approved by the Louisiana Senate and approved by the House with only three dissents. The law was signed by our Governor Jindal, who holds a Bachelor of Science degree (in biology) [N1]. This law allows the teaching of Creationism in Louisiana's public schools under the guise of fostering critical thinking skills. [N2]
    [Nailnote 1] And I've been poking fun at Texans!
    [Nailnote 2] I think I have all the skills necessary to criticize this law in one word. To quote my favorite comedian, Lewis Black, FOSSIL, FOSSIL, FOSSIL, FOSSIL!!!!
9   Which is an ACRONYM for Never Underestimate This Rodent's Insatiable Appetite. If you think I'm full of Texas bovine byproducts or short on science like our legislature check out Louisiana's Wildlife and Fisheries' website at www.Nutria.com where the following appears: *The growing nutria population now has become a serious threat to Louisiana coastal wetlands. The continued increase in nutria will most certainly transform marshlands into open water. It is estimated that approximately 23, 000 acres of wetlands are presently impacted by nutria. The chance of restoring or even slowing the degradation of coastal marshes in Louisiana will be hampered considerably without sustained reduction in nutria impacts.* Nutria made the International Union for the Conservation of Nature's Invasive Species List as one of the top 100 worst invasive species in the world. Boudreaux D. Nutria [T2] and his wife Clotile are also the mascots of the New Orleans'

matter, knows that ever since the first nutria escaped from Old Man McIlhenny's Avery Island pepper farm in the 1930s Southeast Louisiana's wetlands have been steadily declining. After several hours of study and a case of longnecks, we have a plan to save the City of New Orleans, restore the coast of Southeast Louisiana, and at the same time stimulate the local and national economies. The plan is this:

As part of the Obama Administration's new economic stimulus package the federal government must place a sizeable bounty[10] on nutria and create a new faith-based cabinet level position and related bureaucracy under the Secretary of Nutria Extermination and Coastal Restoration (SECNECR) whose primary responsibility would be to:

A.  Convince Archbishop Alfred Hughes[11] to reopen the closed churches to feed the homeless a high-protein nutria diet.

B.  Create jobs for these reinvigorated homeless by restoring the fur business (there aren't any nutria saviors around here).

C.  Turn our armed and dangerous drug dealers into productive nutria-slaughtering tax-paying citizens (the taxes would be withheld as the bounties are paid).

D.  Nutria would also provide a welcome change in diet for those Cajuns who don't already eat them. Everything a Cajun eats tastes like seafood because it is. Of course this presents a conundrum. Since a nutria spends most of its time in water and has webbed rear feet, isn't it seafood? In any event the preparation of nutria would give our great

---

Zephyrs Triple A baseball team.

[Toenote 2] To paraphrase Jeff Foxworthy, if your name is Boudreaux you might be a COONASS! [N3]

[Nailnote 3] You might also be a COONASS if you would take the time and trouble to write a book so you could poke fun at Texans and jerk their halters!

10  If you're going to throw money at something, it might as well be a nutria! The current bounty is $4.00 per nutria which is woefully inadequate and won't get any self-respecting COONASS excited enough to fire up his pirogue—let alone a six-figure drug dealer to fire off his assault rifle.

11  It is rumored that the Archbishop has an identical twin, Howard, a former Munchkin understudy, who is now working as an elf for Keebler.

chefs a challenge to create new gastronomic delicacies (e.g. Nutria Creole and Rice, Nutria Grillades and Grits, Nutria Sauce Piquante, Nutria and Andouille Gumbo, Nutria and Noodles, and the piece de resistance—Daube Glacé a la Nutria).[12] These new recipes would spin off a whole chain of Al Copeland style restaurants, e.g. THE NUTRI-A-DELI with mottos like: So NUTRI-cious, So DELI-cious, It's not just for Gators anymore! (NUTRIA would give a whole new meaning to the term FAST FOOD.)[13]

E.    Encourage free trade by exporting Nutria teeth to China for fabrication into Mardi Gras beads for re-import to New Orleans.

F.    Save Louisiana's coastal marshes from further consumption by nutria and consequential erosion.

G.    Encourage artists to design a whole new line of "T" shirts to be pedaled in the French Quarter by our Pakistani merchants with catchy phrases like *Save Our Coast, Eat a Nutria!* or *Eat More Nutria, Save a Possum!* and *Don't Save the Nutria!* and embellished with drawings of the cute furry critter in the middle, orange incisors and all.

---

12  For additional recipes, including Heart Healthy "Crock Pot" Nutria check www.nutria.com.

13  *Although appearing awkward, the nutria is capable of fast overland travel for considerable distances.*  See www.nutria.com (biology section)

H.     Provide funding to the new Tulane, LSU, VA Medical and Bioscience Research Conglomerate in Central City to genetically engineer a reduction in the size of the nutria to that of a field mouse which could then be managed by domestic house cats. This is a WIN, WIN, WIN, WIN, WIN, WIN, WIN, WIN proposition (someone please call Mary Landrieu and leave a message for David Vitter at Jeanette's on Canal or Norma's on Conti.)[14] If our Nutria Extermination and Coastal Restoration Plan fails Texas could be used as an inexhaustible source of fill dirt and manure to turn Southeast Louisiana into the *Humongous Organic Garden of the United States of America*, hereinafter the *HOG of the USA*,[15] which will rival the Central Valley of California (and we have Ol' Man River for irrigation).

Carnival and particularly Mardi Gras are all about fun and what's more fun than criticizing our politicians and institutions. In fact, our First Amendment rights of free speech and religion identify us as Americans and make us the envy of all freedom-loving people. Nowhere else in the world are these freedoms more freely practiced and jealously guarded than in New Orleans at Carnival time.

Our parade themes frequently cross conventional lines of propriety, good taste, and political correctness for the sake of payback or a good laugh at the expense of a deserving politician or celebrity. The Taboos immediately following the Poem give a taste in written form of what any Carnival spectator is likely to encounter visually as the parade theme unfolds float by float during the procession. For the first time visitor to our Emerald City, as well as Texans, a Glossary of Carnival in New Orleans Terms is provided.

In 2006 New Orleans laughed through its tears as the city and its people decided that, despite the death and destruction wrought by Katrina, Carnival would be celebrated albeit on a smaller scale. Thousands

---

14  If you think you know who Jeanette or Norma are, you're probably right.
15  I served 11 years in the U.S. Navy Reserves and I can spin off ACRONYMS like a hurricane spins off tornadoes!

of evacuees came home for the party and made plans for their eventual return. High school bands, which formerly competed with each other, joined together to form coalitions of musicians[16] which supported the Carnival krewes because in New Orleans we don't dance or parade without music. Some of these kids marched over 40 miles that Carnival week due to the shortage of high school students over five months after the deluge. The success of that season established to the world, and more importantly to New Orleanians, that their city would survive.

In honor of our Katrina survivors and to celebrate our *joie de vivre*, four bonus poems—*Betrayed*, *Katrinaland*, *We're Still Here*, and *So Much for the Bayou*, are included in the *Katrina Poems*. Carnival is full of surprises and there are other surprises throughout the book.

In Louisiana, we call this *lagniappe*—or a little something extra and we hope you enjoy them. (The feds like to blame The Hurricane for the fate of New Orleans and its people. However, it was the failure of a few poorly designed and constructed levees and flood-walls built by the U.S. Army Corps of Engineers that caused the drowning of the city, the destruction of its low-lying areas, and the diaspora of a large population of its poorest people who have been unable to return. With all due respect to action reporters, Richard Angelico, Lee Zurich, and Travers Mackel, after our own brief investigation we were able to put a face on the cause of the near destruction of our beloved city following Katrina—see page 36[17].)

Ever since its founding nearly 300 years ago New Orleans has always been in some form of recovery and we the people of New Orleans have no reason to believe that will ever change nor would we wish it to. As we tell all our visitors, even Texans, *laissez les bon temps rouler*, which means let the good times roll, and they do with each and every Carnival parade. So why don't you fix a drink, relax, and second line with us; remember Bob Seago, John Preble, and I believe <u>that you only</u> live once but, if you do it right, once is enough!

16 The most famous was the MAX Band made up of band members from St. Mary's Academy, St. Augustine High School, and Xavier Prep.

17 Since Katrina our most reliable information is obtained from *The Levee* which boasts *we don't hold anything back* and we feel the same way.

*With this brief background behind us,
on to Carnival in New Orleans....
Key that CD!*

# LET'S ROLL!

# A Prelude to
# Carnival in New Orleans,
# The Poem

Composed Mardi Gras 1989
On a cold, wet, and miserable day
When so consumed by flu and wine
I could not go outside and play.

*The Author*

Uptown and downtown,
All around the
Emerald City,
It's Carnival
in New Orleans
and folks are
feeling silly.

Past and future
generations,
All ages
in between
Have lost their
inhibitions
'Way down in
New Orleans.

The streets are
paved with people
Dressed in
merry masquerade;
"Throw me
something, Mister!"
They cry at
each parade.

Playing catch from
floats by flambeaux,
Krewes are pitching
beads and cups.
On Mardi Gras
Rex and Zulu
Toss doubloons
and coconuts.

Babes are born
from king cakes
Colored purple,
green and gold.
Gay spirits in
The Quarter
Shake and shiver
when it's cold.

Dreamy debutantes
are dancin'
With their beaus
at supper balls;
This time's for
sweet romancin'-
Ripe hearts are
bound to fall.

"My kingdom for a toilet!" Hear his majesty proclaim, "Forget your rules of etiquette, When in my wild domain!"

The late Grand
Duke Alexis
Must be smiling
from above;
And may I be
damned to Texas
If ever I cease to love!

# Purple, Green, and Gold

Purple, Green, and Gold are the official Carnival colors and when applied to a lowly cinnamon roll elevate it to a regal King Cake. (Kind of like kissing a toad, which doesn't always work, but who has actually tried it?) Much ado has been made over the origin of these colors by scholars and pundits, who are not lawyers or elected officials, and thus have no legal authority.[1] Suffice it to say there has been a lot of conjecture and speculation, but no hard proof. To my knowledge there are no state statutes or local ordinances on the subject. Therefore, I suggest this choice of colors must remain a matter of Faith and Morals so like a preacher (who happens to be a lawyer) I feel obliged to share the following:

On a cold December night in 1996, after a particularly long night of hard drinking and loud music, I had a dream that the late Grand Duke Alexis appeared to inform me, in case I wanted to know, that his favorite colors were Purple, Green and Gold. So unless you have seen or heard from the Grand Duke since, I have the latest word, AMEN![2]

# A New Orleans Limerick

There once was a woman named Marilyn
Whose boobs were augmented with paraffin
At the stroke of midnight
Her nipples she'd light
And she'd twinkle from Chalmette to Carrollton.

*To view a picture of Marilyn engaged in her Mardi Gras activities see page 27.*

---

1   Errol Laborde in his new book, *Krewe, The Early New Orleans Carnival Comus to Zulu,* devotes an entire chapter (No.5) to postulate an elaborate heraldic theory of the origin of these colors but his speculation is not based on firsthand knowledge like my information.

2   Amen is short for the phrase—*This is a matter of Faith and Morals, so don't confuse me with the facts, I've made up my mind!*

# The Taboos

*When I was growing up along the **Sliver by the River** near Audubon Park someone told me never to discuss religion, politics, sex, weight, drinking, or nudity in polite company.[1] Since I have no idea if any of my readers can meet this test I feel compelled to briefly mention the following:*

## Religion

By the time New Orleans was founded in 1718 the Spanish Inquisition was pretty much on the wane so no Native Americans were burned at the stake for worshiping the *Great Spirit*. Also New Orleans was one of the few places on Earth the Jewish people hadn't wandered into, although to be perfectly frank New Orleans at that time was anything but the *Promised Land*. However that failure has never been an obstacle in Jewish history, as Jewish tribes have frequently wandered into other garden spots like Egypt, Poland, and Russia. In the early days if you were going to New Orleans you had to go by boat as there was no interstate highway system. Other than some light sport fishing[2] on the Sea of Galilee, the Jews had limited maritime experience and no fleet until the Miami Yacht Club was founded in 1927. Even the Bible verifies this. Moses was found in a basket in the bull rushes, not in a boat, and Jesus, the most famous Jew of all, didn't need a boat because he could walk on water.

---

1   If you can prove you're polite company you can skip this section, but I bet you can't and you won't.[T1]

   [Toenote 1] Gee, I guess I should have put this footnote on the first page.

2   Historically, the Jews weren't great fishermen either, as they relied upon Jesus to feed the masses (remember the loaves and fishes), as opposed to our Vietnamese immigrants[T2] who have never come home from a fishing trip empty-handed or without a seagull or two lashed to the deck.

   [Toenote 2] Since our Vietnamese community in New Orleans has grown (to the point that a native Vietnamese, Representative Cao, was elected to Congress), our Cajuns have learned a thing or two about foraging. In fact, the feral cat population has been decimated in Gentilly. The political opponents of U.S. Rep. Cao have started a rumor that he intends to repeal the leash law, then it's going to be every dog for himself!

Despite hardship the Jews always took time out to party, even inventing the first gambling device—the dreidel. In fact they were the original party animals and never passed up an opportunity (some of which lasted for days) to light candles, drink wine, and eat a lot of food. (No wonder they love New Orleans.) In the old, old days[3] their partying got out of control and, according to the Old Testament, Yahweh had to correct them on several occasions finally handing them His Ten Commandments to live by or else.

The answer to the question, *Who are God's chosen people?*, has always been the *Jews*. However, the answer to the follow-up question, *Chosen for what?*, remains a mystery. *Now moving on to politics...*

# Politics

Our politicians have become famous for using and abusing the *Five Most Feared Words* in the English language especially against their opponents in election campaigns, *I'll get you my pretty!* This is particularly true of our female politicians. In its 292+ year history New Orleans, like Oz, has never had a shortage of brainless scarecrows, heartless tinmen, cowardly lions, sundry witches, and various voodoo queens.[4] New Orleans once had a police chief named Eddie Compass who didn't know where he was going or where he had been and couldn't follow the *Yellow Brick Road* even if we had one.

Louisiana's former congressman, Bill Jefferson, from the 2nd Congressional District (and Rep. Cao's predecessor), fondly known as *Dollar Bill* by his constituents, was recently convicted of 11 out of 16 felony counts[5] by the Federal District Court in Alexandria, VA. After the verdict I imagined that Mr. Jefferson reportedly said, and I quote, *When I was growing up the white politicians were the crooks but they didn't get caught. Here I am a poor black man with only $90,000.00*

---

3   Using the Jewish calendar we are in the year 5770.
4   To my young readers these are not gay magicians or musicians, but real black artists like Marie Laveau.
5   Now that all the crooks are using cell phones the Feds ought to change their indictments to *wireless* fraud.

*in my freezer, and I've been convicted—this isn't about political corruption, this is about equal protection.*[6]

A few months ago there was a rumor circulating around that Tulane's world famous Primate Center on the Northshore had received a federal grant to partner with the Department of Defense to clone a new species of flying monkey to replace our unmanned combat drones in Iraq.[7] However the program was scrapped after Rumsfeld escaped, and W retired to Crawford.[8] *Now moving on to Sex....*

## Sex

Our visitors should know that some of our New Orleans residents don't always wait for Mardi Gras to dress up. Awhile ago a handsome young cowboy (from Texas, not Brokeback Mountain in Wyoming) thought he was in Europe, instead of New Orleans, and wanted to take a Mediterranean Cruise across the river to Algiers. He approached what appeared to be an overdressed streetwalker and asked, *Pardon me* <u>*ma'am, but*</u> *where can I*

6  With an African American President in the White House who just appointed an Hispanic Justice to the U.S. Supreme Court, I do not believe this argument will prevail on appeal.

7  If you want to see how effective these monkeys can be you should rent the Wizard of Oz from Blockbuster.

8  W always reminded me of Curious George. (W has that deer-in-headlights expression, but without the curious affect.)

*find the Canal Street Ferry?* With a limp wrist and a breathless sigh, the drag queen responded, *Why honey, you're looking at him!*

In support of President Obama's economic policy I created my own stimulus package. I filled prescriptions for Viagra and Testosterone and hired a belly dancer[9] to replace my old secretary. *Now moving on to Weight...*

# Size (Weight)[10]

No discussion about size or weight would be complete without mentioning some of our king-size citizens who are scattered throughout various parts of the city. Take for example Gobblekins who reside with Chalmations[11] in St. Bernard Parish. The Gobblekins' size is related to their diet which consists of too many hot plate lunches at Rocky & Carlo's,[12] where the house salad is macaroni and cheese with brown or red gravy dressing, and late-night po-boys which are gobbled[13] like Junior Leaguers down cucumber finger sandwiches. Gobblekins are to New Orleans what Munchkins are to the Emerald City with one obvious difference. Although both talk funny, Munchkins are little people whereas Gobblekins are quite a bit larger than the average size New Orleanian (unless you are a Saints offensive lineman).

Here's how to tell the difference between a normal Chalmation and a Gobblekin, other than size. If you stand up in the morning, can see your feet, and notice white shrimp boots, chances are you are a Chalmation. If you stand before your 36" wide door mirror, and still <u>have to move</u> side to side to see your whole body the chances are

9 She can be reached at www.bellydanceneworleans.com but she won't perform in Texas because she's afraid of rattlesnakes.
10 WARNING- There is a lot of sophomoric humor in this section but with all of New Orleans' high schools and colleges I believe the audience to be more than adequate.
11 Chalmations lik ta tink d'er from N'Awlins but d'er not. D'er from da Parish (St. Bernard) where Benny Grunch and Da Bunch and Da Po'Boys hang out.
12 Rocky & Carlo's, Chalmette's most famous restaurant, boasts of serving 1,000 lbs. of macaroni and 1,000 lbs. of cheese per week to its customers. Annually, this amounts to 183,040,000 calories without accounting for the gravy dressing, the main course, or dessert. (No wonder Southeast Louisiana is subsiding.)
13 The etiology of the term *Gobblekins*.

you are a Gobblekin. If packages of leftovers in your icebox[14] have individual names or initials printed in Marks-A-Lot, chances are you are a Chalmation. If your icebox has no leftovers, chances are you are a Gobblekin. If you eat more that three meals a day at Rocky & Carlo's or have a reserved space in their parking lot then you might be a Gobblekin. Finally, if you need a full-size SUV to haul your butt around, you're probably a Gobblekin.

Gobblekins are characterized by a voracious appetite accompanied by loud sucking[15] sounds which create low pressure systems[16] near their lips that are autonomic responses to boiling crustaceans,[17] shucking ersters,[18] and tapping beer kegs.

In a large enclosed space in Chalmette, like the Chalmette Cultural Center,[19] the sound of Gobblekins feasting (when they are not talking over each other, because their talking mechanisms are disengaged while eating) rivals that of a squadron of airboats at full throttle over the marsh, or the decibel level on any Friday afternoon at Galatoires' when the lawyers arrive after the Civil District Court shuts down.[20]

After Katrina, St. Tammany Parish had a huge influx of Chalmations as St. Bernard Parish was completely inundated. Local trial lawyers were excited about it because Chalmations don't pay attention to traffic signals or stop signs,[21] flip people off, and cause lots of accidents. However, because they all have minimal insurance coverage and no seizable assets that anyone would want, the excite-

---

14 This is Chalmation for refrigerator.
15 This is the first documented use of the phrase *pinching tails* and *sucking heads* without sexual implications, and yet another twist to the term *deep throat*.
16 At times these systems have even triggered the Storm Alert Radar on Bob Breck's weather advisory.
17 Shrimp, crabs, or crawfish
18 This is Chalmation for oysters.
19 The most outrageous oxymoron in Louisiana history rivaling the Harahan Historical Society.
20 New Orleans lawyers are never out-talked or out-eaten by their clients with the exception of the Gobblekins in Chalmette and a few particularly healthy coonasses near Breaux Bridge.
21 If you happen to stop first at a four-way stop, Chalmations consider they have pre-empted the right-of-way.

ment quickly wore off. After Katrina St. Tammany residents encountered bumper stickers on Chalmation vehicles which read *Welcome to St. Tammanard Darlin* with a graphic of a cute pair of white rubber shrimp boots.[22] In retaliation to this cultural faux pas I created some king-sized bumper stickers for Gobblekin SUVs.

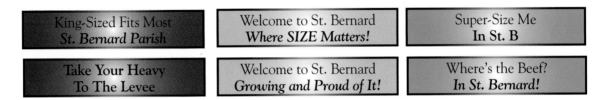

| | | |
|---|---|---|
| King-Sized Fits Most *St. Bernard Parish* | Welcome to St. Bernard *Where SIZE Matters!* | Super-Size Me **In St. B** |
| Take Your Heavy To The Levee | Welcome to St. Bernard *Growing and Proud of It!* | Where's the Beef? *In St. Bernard!* |

The day Chalmations start worrying about exercise and diet, so they won't become Gobblekins, will be the same day they rename Judge Perez Drive Martin Luther King, Jr. Blvd.!

No book about Carnival or New Orleans would be complete without a discussion of our favorite liquid, *now moving on to....*

# Booze

New Orleans is a place where alcohol permeates the aquifer which recharges the fountain of youth underlying the city. So that by 2a.m., after a long evening of drinking, a toothless hag mutates into a movie star, and a paunchy, balding 50 year old guy is transformed into an Olympic athlete. Our methods of dispensing alcohol in New Orleans measure up to the distribution of drinking water via any municipal water system in America. With more bars per capita than any other place and no curfews other than one prohibiting street drinking after 12a.m. on one day of the year (Ash Wednesday– the official end

---

22 When Chalmations shop at Wal-Mart they are sometimes confused with Wal-Mations until their dialect and white shrimp boots give them away.

of Mardi Gras), the booze flows in New Orleans 24/7 like the Mississippi River flows to the Gulf with annual floods (inside the levees) on major holidays, Saints home games, LSU championships, and Mardi Gras. And if some barrooms are closed (probably because the sun is out while most drunks, bartenders, and vampires[23] are sleeping in) then the drugstores, the grocery stores, and the liquor stores can quench any thirst any time behind the veil of a brown paper bag.

New Orleans is also full of Daiquiri Shops with drive-up/drive thru windows where plastic lids cover the cup contents and a porthole is provided for the insertion of a straw. Because the straw provided is delivered in a separate wrapper, unconnected to the container, this practice does not constitute a violation of the Open Container law. This exhibits one of New Orleans' famous dichotomies; when faced with an obvious temptation our legislators trust us more than we trust them![24]

New Orleans allows open containers and street drinking in the French Quarter, but only if your drinks are in plastic containers. This makes perfect sense. You don't want your visitors cut to shreds by broken glass when they pass out face-down in the gutter.

In New Orleans the health and safety of our visitors is always our number one priority, and of course drugs and alcohol have nothing to do with our proclivity to shoot each other at the least provocation.[25] The Dueling Oaks in City Park attest to the fact that the New Orleans tradition of firing pistols at one another over *affaires d'honneur* dates back to the 18th century.

In the interest of trade and commerce the Tourist Commission recently circulated a bulletin requesting that our drug dealers take extra precaution not to inadvertently wing any tourists[26] during exchanges of automatic weapon fire at turf battles.

<u>       </u> *Finally, we get to that most prohibited subject of all.... Nudity*

23  Anne Rice made millions from her vampire series so don't tell me that no one believes in vampires in New Orleans.
24  To quote the Church Lady, that fount of modern moral rectitude, *Well, isn't that special!*
25  Which often starts with rhetorical questions like, *What did you say!* [T1]
    [Toenote 1] This does not mean that the provocateur has a hearing problem.
26  Lest they kill the goose etc.....

26 breasoning

# Marilyn Goes to Mardi Gras

Marilyn heads to the French Quarter bead balconies with her bead magnets exposed—soon to be targets for ring toss and big hits with the bead throwers.
*Photo by the Author, Mardi Gras 1984, French Quarter*

## Nudity (Obscenity)

On Mardi Gras we encourage costuming. In other places it's against the law to wear a mask or conceal your identity, particularly while robbing a liquor store. Depending on the weather and temperature in New Orleans, *costuming* to some means wearing little more than their birthday suit adorned with body paint, beads, and a codpiece. As the old saying goes, *beauty is in the eye of the beholder* and the same rule goes for obscenity. The U.S. Supreme Court has

held that whether or not something is obscene is to be judged by community standards. So what's acceptable in the French Quarter might occasion SHOCK AND AWE in the Garden District. Knowing what or what not to wear and where or where not to go dressed like that are important decisions on Mardi Gras, lest you offend the local *gendarmes* and earn a free ride in a paddy wagon, which may be disguised as a Carnival float. Suffice it to say—if everyone is decently dressed where you are and children are present behave yourself. However if you are in a place where articles of clothing have been removed and only consenting adults are present, then you should feel free to remove the identical items—at least if you earn that free ride you won't be alone and you might meet some interesting people.

One important word of advice; do not curse, berate, argue with, or ignore the Eighth District NOPD officers who are highly trained and experienced in crowd control and management of the surly and the unruly. The free exercise of your First Amendment rights in this context could easily result in the wholesale violation of your Fourth Amendment rights which in the best case scenario will ruin your Mardi Gras experience. Remember these three words and you should have no trouble with the cops, who after all are not having a great time watching everyone else having a great time, ALWAYS BE POLITE![27]

## A WARNING TO PARENTS:

Don't take your children to the French Quarter on Mardi Gras. When they are old enough they will find it by themselves. Then, hopefully, they won't run into you in the same barroom.

---

27 I recommend that you never try to kiss or hug a cop (even of the opposite sex) unless the cop is off-duty and in the same condition you find yourself. [T1]
[Toenote 1] Even then because of leadership training I'd let the cop make the first move unless you have your own handcuffs.

# Oops, I Almost Forgot

## *Jefferson Parish*

The real reason I haven't mentioned Jefferson Parish until now is I almost forgot. However, on second thought, it doesn't deserve mention other than as a Shopping Mecca subject to spending pilgrimages,[1] traffic jams, and parking lots.

Jefferson Parish was named after one of our greatest Presidents, Thomas Jefferson, but other than that it has little to recommend it particularly since gambling was legalized. When I was a kid my best friend's father used to take us behind the levee at Shrewsbury to shoot our 22 rifles. Today you would be arrested for doing that. When I was in high school we used to go dove hunting at the end of David Drive on Lake Ponchartrain in an old pasture full of ragweed. Between sneezes we would shoot our limit. In college we drove across The Huey P.[2] (which is still scary to me) to the Westwego[3] grain elevators to shoot doves from the top of the levee. So Jefferson Parish, to me, has always been a place to fire a gun, which can't hold a candle to Orleans Parish these days.

The only character who ever came out of Jefferson worth mentioning was Sheriff Harry Lee[4] who was not related to General Robert E. Lee[5] even within six degrees of separation. However, based upon some of his public comments which provoked the attention of the NAACP, the outspoken Sheriff Lee may have thought his parish was named after Jefferson Davis—another great President. Sheriff Lee was also known as quite a dove hunter himself and, although he had a keen shooting eye, he never seemed to recognize a baited field especially when he was hunting in one which provoked the attention

---

1   It has been blamed for killing Canal Street as a shopping destination and encouraged a Katrina-like permanent evacuation of middle class whites to the suburbs in the 60s and 70s.

2   A high, long, and narrow bridge over the Mississippi River built in 1935

3   One of the most entertaining names for a small town which Horace Greely would approve.

4   Sheriff Lee has a life-size statue erected in his memory on Veterans Blvd., where most Jefferson parades are viewed, with the Sheriff holding a 10 gallon hat in his right hand (from Texas of all places- this is really scary!)

5   Harry Lee was a Chinese Lee not a Confederate Lee.

of the *Federales* (these are U.S. Fish and Wildlife Game Wardens).

By the way, since I don't hunt there anymore, and Sheriff Lee is gone, I understand the dove population in Jefferson is out of control. The Jeffersonians always brag that they are *on the move*, but I don't know where. Most people on the move these days move to the Northshore bypassing Jefferson altogether.

# Northshorians

Where do you live? she asked.

*The Northshore.* he replied.

The north shore of what?

*The north shore of Lake of Pontchartrain.*

Is that a town?

*No, we used to live in small towns and villages*
*Like Slidell, Lacombe, Mandeville, Madisonville,*
*Abita Springs, Covington, and Folsom*
*But they are all gone now—*
*Enveloped by urban sprawl,*
*Connected by subdivisions,*
*And glued together with fast food.*

Well then, what do you call yourselves?

*I guess you could call us Northshorians.*

Northshorians?

*Yes, people who've lost their identity.*

# The Katrina Poems

## Betrayed

(Katrina, August 29,2005)

## Katrinaland

(One Year Later)

## We're Still Here

(Three Years Later)

## So Much for the Bayou

(Forevermore)

New Orleans —

NASA's Earth Observatory
August 29, 2005

# Betrayed

We used to love our hurricanes.
In their honor we declared holidays,
Taped our windows, cleared our yards,
Bought batteries and candles,
Called our friends,
Evacuated to local bars,
And had a ball!

Sure the streets flooded
But we had pumps.
Sure the waves rolled
But we had levees.
With Nash on TV,
The nuns on their beads,
And a drink in our hands
We were prepared!

Betsy in '65, Camille in '69
Were but faded memories
When along came Katrina;
A storm on steroids-
Stronger than Betsy,
Bigger than Camille,
Impervious to pumps, levees, and prayers;
She washed our love away!

August 29, 2005
Katrina Makes Landfall

# Washed Away

This NOAA photo is of the Mississippi Gulf Coast following Katrina. The Gulf Coast was in the Northeast quadrant of the storm where the winds and storm surge were at their worst and wreaked total destruction. Like some parts of New Orleans, the Mississippi Gulf Coast is still struggling to come back almost four years after the storm.

# Katrinaland

We live in Katrinaland, in the State of Discombobulation,
The new territory carved out in the wakes of Katrina and Rita,
Which stretches from Pascagoula to Port Arthur,
And up to 150 miles inland from the coast.
New Orleans is its capital.
In Katrinaland, everything spins counterclockwise
In slow motion from the storms' impact.

In this no-man's land, there are too many people,
Too many trucks, too much trash, debris, and smoke
Too many contractors, yet not enough contractors,
And a scarcity of trees, homes, bridges, and highways.
Here, queuing up is a way of life.  Patience is passé.
Medication, whether prescribed or not, is a necessity,
And everyone needs treatment but the doctors are gone.

Here, the attention span is measured in milliseconds,
And the obituary column is measured in feet.
Here, the checks are in the mail but the post office is closed,
And the help that is promised never comes.
Here, we stagger through each day like Joe Palooka on the ropes
Waiting and sometimes praying for that final knockout punch.
In Katrinaland, everyone wonders but no one knows,

*What the hell is going on?*

August 29, 2006
One year later

# AHOLA[1] OF NOLA
### (The eagle has landed!)

## COL. I.M. FUBAR

U.S. Army Corps of Engineers (Ret.)
On leave in the French Quarter for Mardi Gras
(On this occasion Col. Fubar was cited by the NOMP for being out of uniform)
*Photo by Author, Mardi Gras 1984, French Quarter*

---

1 AHOLA of NOLA: acronym for Army's Head of Levee Assessment for the district of New Orleans, LA. This is the man responsible for the poor design of the Seventeenth St., London Ave., and Industrial Canal levees which failed after the city survived Katrina. Before beginning his military career Col. Fubar [T1] worked as a tool pusher and heavy equipment operator with Texaco.

[Toenote 1] FUBAR is a famous military acronym relating to a identity crisis. [N1]

    [Nailnote 1] Col. Fubar is not to be confused with Major Snafu, his second-in-command, the guy in the chicken hat on Col. Fubar's right (stage left). [N2]

    [Nailnote 2] Check out the longhorn loafers on Maj. Snafu. Could the levee failures have been part of a larger Texas-based conspiracy—we should get our action reporters on this immediately!

# We're Still Here

Dedicated to real "Survivors," the People of New Orleans

Let wind and rain and hurricane blow –
But we're still here.
Everyone knows that levee's too low –
But we're still here.
When help might come we'll never know –
But we're still here.

There's no place we'd rather go
Than at sea level or just below.
Some say we're silly but we're sincere –
You just can't know 'till you've lived here.
So FEMA can come and FEMA can go
But we're still here.

Let's raise a toast to our good cheer –
If no champagne we'll just drink beer;
Pray for high pressure and skies to clear –
No matter what storms come 'round next year
Below CAT-4 we have no fear,
'Cause we'll still be here.

August 29, 2008
Three years later

# So Much for the Bayou

The sky is so much bluer,
The breeze is so much cooler,
The grass is so much  greener,
The earth is so much cleaner,
The stars are so much brighter,
Our cares are so much lighter,
No matter what the weather,
Our days are so much better,
On the bayou.[1]

Forevermore.

---

1   As this book goes to press, Mike the Bayou Bengal mascot of LSU, has just turned
    Bevo, the Longhorn mascot of the University of Texas, into Boudin at the 2009 College
    World Series in Omaha, Nebraska. How sweet it is! Life is good on the bayou! [T1]
    [Toenote 1] The legendary rivarly between the Coonasses and the Jackasses continues. [N1]
    [Nailnote 1] In New Orleans we love to Mess with Texas!

# A Riddle of Mardi Gras Mythology

Question: What mythological Goddess
sprung fully formed from the head of Zulu?

*Answer page 71*

# Epilogue

Like all Carnival revelers before me I have tried to poke fun at everyone with equanimity. To date I have targeted White Men, Texans, Cajuns, Jews, Catholics[1] (from the humble nun on her beads to the very vaults of the Vatican), Fundamental Christians, Pakistani Muslims, African-Americans, rednecks, Mexicans, Vietnamese, Chalmations, Jeffersonians, Northshorians, politicians of every persuasion including a former New Orleans Police Chief, the NOPD, a Jefferson Parish Sheriff, Louisiana Legislators, the Mayor of New Orleans, the Governor of Louisiana, the Secretary of Defense, the US Army Corps of Engineers, the President and Vice President of the United States, U.S. Senators Landrieu and Vitter, and in no particular order or hierarchy, the gay community, the homeless, the Saints, dwarfs, the obese, lawyers and judges, cats and dogs, seagulls, and last but not least, the poor nutrias.[2] If for some reason I missed you or your group I apologize; the snub was unintentional. Please let me know and I promise I will make it up to you the next time I have the opportunity.[3]

---

1   By definition, Cajuns and Catholics are usually one and the same so there's a double dose of fun.

2   Who were perfectly happy in South America until they were captured and brought here against their will by the nutria traders.

3   Please don't send me any lawyer jokes. I've heard them all and written several myself, like:
    Q: Do you know how to get a lawyer down from a tree?
    A: *Cut the rope.*
(I once used this joke in a voir dire to a predominately black jury in Civil District Court in Orleans Parish and thereafter obtained a favorable verdict for my two white clients—*Dennis v. Dry Klean Carpet Maintenance, Co., et al.*)

# Glossary

**Babe:** a small plastic doll which is buried in each King Cake before cutting and serving the pieces; the unlucky recipient of the babe has to buy the next King Cake

**Beau:** the male counterpart of belle; a handsome boyfriend

**Belle:** a young and attractive single female

**Boudin:** a Cajun sausage made from pork rice dressing (much like dirty rice) which is stuffed into pork casings. It is normally simmered or braised, although coating with oil and slow grilling for tailgating is becoming a popular option in New Orleans and Baton Rouge

**Carnival:** from Carne Vale—O flesh, farewell! The season of merrymaking before Lent

**Cat-4:** an abbreviation for a category 4 hurricane with sustained winds from 131-155mph

**Coonass:** a jackass east of the Sabine River

**Debutante:** a young woman who is being introduced to polite society by her parents through the coming-out parties of the Carnival organizations in which she may participate as a maid or a queen; being chosen the Queen of Carnival is the highest honor bestowed on any young lady making her debut

**Doubloon:** colored metal coin usually stamped with the krewe's name and date of parade, which is a treasured Carnival throw (originated with the Krewe of Rex in 1960)

**Emerald City:** the capital of Oz and the most appropriate handle for New Orleans because both places are fantasy dream states

**FEMA:** Federal Emergency Management Agency; the agency in charge of the federal government's disaster relief program

**Huey P. Long Bridge:** named after Louisiana's notorious U.S. Senator and ex-populist Governor, Huey P. Long, who was preparing to run for President of the United States when he was assassinated inside of the state capitol in Baton Rouge on September 8, 1935; it was the first bridge built over the Mississippi River in Louisiana which opened in December 1935. The bridge is known for it's steep and narrow 9' wide road lanes without shoulders, where trucks are prohibited from passing each other. The bridge is still in service and is scheduled for renovation and widening of its travel lanes in 2013.

**Jackass:** a coonass west of the Sabine River

**Joie de vivre:** the joy of living. Don't forget the French are all about life—their favorite cheer being *Vive la France!* the principal word here being Vivre, because without *Vivre* you can't have *Joie*. When Thomas Jefferson purchased Louisiana from Napoleon in 1803, most of the indigenous population was French. The French believe that you don't do anything to risk your *vie*, which explains why the predominantly French-American citizens of the city of New Orleans, when faced with the overwhelming might of the Yankee fleet on the Mississippi River during the Civil War, decided that prudence dictated surrender particularly since they were surrendering to their former country which wasn't all that bad anyway. Besides the French are known for making love, not war. (With a name like Maurice Le Gardeur, no one can doubt I know what I'm talking about. There's that rhyming problem again.)

**Judge Perez Drive:** originally named after Judge Leander Perez, a notorious political boss and staunch white supremacist/segregationist who opposed the integration of the public schools in the 60's. He tried to intimidate white Catholics to oppose Archbishop Rummel's plans to integrate the Catholic schools in his district. For this action Archbishop Rummel excommunicated Perez from the church, whereupon Perez announced that he would create his own church- the Perezbyterians. Under pressure to repudiate Leander's influence the St. Bernard Parish council re-

dedicated Judge Perez Drive to Judge Melvin Perez, so they wouldn't have to go to the expense of changing the road signs. (As the Church Lady used to say on Saturday Night Live, *How conveeeenient!*)

**King Cake:** a cinnamon breakfast roll shaped in a ring, sometimes stuffed with filling which is adorned with purple, green, and gold, sugar and icing, and sold seasonally between Twelfth Night and Mardi Gras by all local groceries and bakeries

**Krewe:** a Carnival organization of private members who put on a parade at their own expense *pro bono publico* or for the good of the public free of charge

**Nash:** Nash Roberts, also known as "The Weather God," was the WDSU Channel 6 weatherman from 1948-1973 whose accurate storm forecasts were legendary even without modern day radar and satellite scanning

**Rex:** the King of Carnival who rules New Orleans on Mardi Gras and who receives the keys to the city from the Wizard/Mayor at Gallier Hall

**Second Line:** Bystanders form a second line to follow a marching band alongside the participants so that in effect you join the procession and prolong the musical experience. Common at Carnival parades and jazz funerals (upon leaving the cemetery). The identity of the dearly departed is of no concern to the bystanders—the musical procession presents a serendipitous occasion for a good time beginning with the jazz classic, *Oh, Didn't He Ramble!*

**The Quarter:** short for the Vieux Carre' (the Old Square); now known as the French Quarter; the original footprint of the city of New Orleans, the center of which is Jackson Square; the Quarter is bounded by Canal, Basin, Esplanade, and the Mississippi River

**Wizard (of Oz):** also known as the Mayor of New Orleans

**Zulu:** a primarily African-American Carnival Krewe (which also parades on Mardi Gras) known for throwing decorated spears and coconuts, originally created as a parody of the Rex organization

# Illustrations by Robert Seago

**Front cover:** Three dukes on horseback escort the King's float in the traditional Carnival colors

**Page xii:** New Orleans Landmarks

**Page xviii:** Nutria drawing by W. Kuhnert

**Page 3:** The King's Jester—Rex's large papier-mache court jester who follows the king's float and who bears a striking resemblance to Kriss Fairbairn, the WDSU TV Channel 6 news anchor who also has an infectious smile

**Page 5:** Humpty Dumpty on Parade—one of the many fantasy and fairy-tale characters commonly depicted on Carnival floats whose subjects vary annually depending on parade themes

**Page 7:** *Throw Me Something Mister!*—the most frequent cry heard during Carnival season in New Orleans as crowds beg beads and other favors from the masked float riders who frequently seek favors in return (like a peek at Marilyn's bead magnets).

**Page 9:** Flambeaux Carriers—carry kerosene lanterns with multiple wicks aloft on a pole, the butt of which rests in a leather harness at the waist of the carrier; flambeaux traditionally illuminated night parades before floats were wired with electric generators. Some old line krewes still sparingly use flambeaux to the consternation of the fire department.

**Page 11:** The Boeuf Gras—the fatted calf; Carnival symbol of feasting which precedes Ash Wednesday and the beginning of Lent when most diets in New Orleans begin in earnest (the day to which most New Year's resolutions are postponed).

**Page 13:** Carnival Ball Maskers—traditionally the krewe members mask for the balls and present a tableau or brief performance based on a theme before the ball begins. Thereafter ladies are called out

to the dance floor by committee members in formal dress where they dance with their masked and allegedly anonymous partners. Following this dance the masker usually bestows a favor on his lady friend—a trinket or souvenir as a memento of the occasion.

*All of the illustrations and photos in this book, including the cover, plus a full poster poem of Carnival in New Orleans and other images of New Orleans and Louisiana are available at www.artcardsnola.com*

# Momus Toasts His Queen

Momus toasts his queen at the Boston Club on Canal Street. The
Knights of Momus, the third oldest Krewe founded in 1872, is associated
with the Louisiana Club. Momus no longer parades in New Orleans but
continues to stage an annual ball on the Thursday before Fat Tuesday.

# Appendix I

## If Ever I Cease to Love

In a house, in a square, in a quadrant
In a street, in a lane, in a road.

Turn to the left on the right hand
You see there my true love's abode

I go there a courting, and cooing to my love like a dove;
And swearing on my bended knee, If Ever I Cease to Love,
May sheep-heads grow on apple trees, If Ever I Cease to Love.

Chorus:
If Ever I Cease to Love, If Ever I Cease to Love,
May the moon be turn'd to green cream cheese,
If Ever I Cease to Love

She can sing, she can play on the piano,
She can jump, she can dance, she can run.

For she's a wonderful girlie; She's all of that rolled into one.
I adore her beauty, She's like an angel dropped from above;
May the fish get legs and the cows lay eggs
If Ever I Cease to Love

May all dogs wag their tails in front,
If Ever I Cease to Love

Second Chorus:
If Ever I Cease to Love, If Ever I Cease to Love,
May we all turn into cats and dogs,
If Ever I Cease to Love

*Geo. Leybourne, London 1871*

# Appendix II

## New Mardi Gras Classics
*Music and Lyrics by John Preble*
*www.abitianrecords.com*

**16 HITS**

1 Koo Koo La Ba
2 This Is Endymion
3 At The Mardi Gras
4 King Zulu
5 Mardi Gras In Evangeline
6 I See The Parade
7 When The Levees Broke
8 Prettiest Girl On Mardi Gras
9 Do The Mardi Gras
10 Mardi Gras On The Mind
11 Mardi Gras Jones
12 Carnival Memories
13 The King Of Bacchus
14 Mardi Gras Season
15 Orpheus Night
16 Do You Know The King

**FEATURING**
The Abitians
Bobby Lounge
Dash Rip Rock
The Petty Bones

# Koo Koo La Ba

*Vocals By Dyane Mitchell*

It's Saturday night,
it's Mardi Gras, here's what's going on
We go to mid city,
meet our friends for Endymion

It's Sunday night,
it's Mardi Gras, we got it made
I got ladders on St. Charles
for the Bacchus parade

It's Monday night,
it's Mardi Gras, here's what we do

Orpheus, on Napoleon—
yeah that my Krewe

It's Tuesday morning,
I'm feeling beat, but it's Mardi Gras
It's the big day and all I can say is,
"Ku Ku La Ba"

It's Wednesday morning,
it's all over, but just one thing
Go to church see Deacon John,
hear angles sing

# King Zulu

*Vocals By Jerry Hess*

It started in Africa
wound up on Jackson Avenue
It started in Africa
wound up on Jackson Avenue
You see him on that float,
that's my King Zulu

Bring your baby,
but man you better watch her
They got a Big Shot
and a witch doctor
You see him on that float,
that's my King Zulu

The music so loud
you got hold your ears
They be hearin that drum line
all the way in Algiers
They be throwin beads
and them big old spears

We'll party on Jackson
and get all messed up
We'll hear the bands
and watch the big girls strut
I'm gonna gets my baby
a real gold coconut

# I See The Parade

*Performed by Bobby Lounge*

Do you know the king?

Well the City Park Horses,
gonna fly in tune
I see the parades, Lord, a coming soon
And there's a big green trout
in the back lagoon

I saw the Queen
by the China ball tree

Lets all give a hand to the N, O, P, D
Do you know, Lord,
do you know the king?

Ah when I die,
well you can second line
And eulogize me, Lord, all in rhyme
Oh do you know, you know the king?

# This Is Endymion
*Vocals By Jerry Hess*

Anonymous gypsies,
maids and queens
Exploded in light down
in New Orleans
It was brilliant theater,
Bohemian luck,
this is Endymion

The traveling empire's
brief commission
Blessed the crowds
with rogue ambition
I saw civilization collapse,
and erupt again.

CHORUS:
She smiled and looked out to sea,
in waves of moving hands
Looking for her lover,

inside this wonderland
From the float her view was clear,
this feral neutral ground
But that flambeau
who stole her heart,
he was never found

Troubadours rode this wild tableau
With Melpoumeen and Papa Joe
An expedition painted in lights,
this is Endymion

CHORUS

Let every one here raise their glass
To our kings and queens of the past
And to our new host,
I sing to you "this is Endymion"

# Mardi Gras On The Mind
*Performed by the Petty Bones*

Oh goodness gracious
We're gonna have a blast
The car's all packed now
There's a whole full tank of gas
We're driving down South
Everyone will be there
To have a crazy time
It's carnival season
We got Mardi Gras on the mind

Buddy Bob out in Santa Fe
called the other night
He was feeling kind of funky
So booked his Southern flight
He's flying down to party
And join the conga line
It's carnival season
He's got Mardi Gras on the mind

Now Lou's out in LA
She wants a good road trip
Her rig's out on the interstate
She's gonna let it rip
With Al Johnson on the CD
Chasing down that I-10 sign
It's carnival season
She's got Mardi Gras on the mind

All across the USA
You can feel it in the air
It's the Super Bowl of parties
And they all want to be there
So come on everybody
Take it easy and unwind
It's carnival season
They got Mardi Gras on the mind

# Mardi Gras In Evangeline

*Vocals By Jerry Hess*

Chookie plays in a Cajun band
He plays the accordion
They play in Tee Mamou
And Church Point too

On Mardi Gras Chookie and the band
Ride their ponies cross the land
They got their costumes on
Man they cutting it up

CHORUS:
It's Mardi Gras In Evangeline
Everybody's passing a good time
It's Mardi Gras In Evangeline
Everybody's passing a good time

Chookie calls his horse Boudreaux
They're riding for a big gumbo
They got the roosters and rice
And some Cajun spice

Now Mardi Gras comes
just once a year
But Chookie and the boys
are always here
They know where it's at
And that's just lagniappe

# Do The Mardi Gras

*Vocals By Dyane Mitchell*

Kathieeeee
Kathie, wash my car
Kathie, Kathie, wash my car
And you can be my queen
at the Mardi Gras

Gina, Gina, cut my yard
Gina, Gina, cut my yard

And you can be my queen
at the Mardi Gras
Dewey, Dewey, La, La Ba
Ku Ku, Ku Ku, La, La Ba
Come on everybody come on and do
the Mardi Gras

# Orpheus Night

*Performed by Dash Rip Rock*

There's something outside,
out in the air now
It sounds like a tom,
a bass and a snare now
I see police and a flashing light
Looks like we got an Orpheus night

Napoleon's looking extraordinary
With the Trojan horse

and Smokey Mary
And those butterflies are out of sight
Looks like we got an Orpheus night

Let's hit the party
when the parade is done
And join up with Leviathan
We'll dance till we see daylight
And celebrate this Orpheus night

# Mardi Gras Jones

*Vocals By Jerry Hess*

I was birthed at Charity
on Mardi Gras Day
Momma saw me they heard her say
This child it the prettiest I ever seen
One day he's cooler
than the ice machine
Gonna name my baby,
umm humm, she moans
Gonna names that child
Mardi Gras Jones

Rent a house off lower St. Charles
Find me every night
at the Mardi Gras Balls
I go it alone but that's my intention
Late that night I seek
divine intervention
I take my baby to places unknown
I'm the dude, Mardi Gras Jones

I'm getting psyched up for the big day
Worked two jobs, get good pay
Have a silk tie with a monogram
M. G. J., I'm the man

Alligator shoes, musk colognes
I'm the dude, Mardi Gras Jones

Mardi Gras, spend a little dough
Armani suit, a white limo
Have my driver brings me around
Early in the morning I'm in Gert Town
On my ring that ain't rhinestones
I'm the dude called Mardi Gras Jones

I see Indians, and they see me
They run me off cause I'm so pretty
Go see Zulu, on Jackson
I'm the center of all the action
Gots purple green
and gold cell phones
I'm the dude, Mardi Gras Jones

Now when I die I stay above ground
I want to still hear the bands get down
Beads gonna hang around my grave
Friends walk by they all gonna say
In this grave there's more than bones
There lies the dude
called Mardi Gras Jones

# Carnival Memories

*Vocals By Jerry Hess*

My carnival memories sing
out snapshots of you
Your funny dance, your happy shoes
Thank you for the dreams
Sweet Mardi Gras dreams

It's great to look back
to those carnival days
Going out and watching parades,
laughing with the kids
Catching kisses in the air

Oh the costume you wore would
make a peacock jealous
The music you made
you could have been a Marsalis
We had a party everyday
We had a Mardi Gras World

If I were Blain Kern
and you a cotton truck
I paint you Shamrocks
and call you Lady Luck
We had our parade
We had our Mardi Gras World

# The King Of Bacchus

*Vocals By Jerry Hess*

There were grand attendants,
footmen and drivers
One hundred stallions
and one hundred riders
I saw ushers escorting
their imperial guests
Surveyed the crowds
I spied a million at best
The florescent archangels strolled
As the King of Bacchus rolled

Chalices of plastic
burst through the night
From a pneumatic cannon
to the crowd's delight
I saw tubas of gold
and white fiberglass
I danced with a child
as St. Augustine passed
And the arc lights beamed out of control
The King of Bacchus rolled

# Mardi Gras Season

Vocals By Jerry Hess

It's beginning to be that time, that season
We'll throw away all normalcy and reason
There's a king cake party in Gentilly
Your new costume is big time silly
It's Mardi Gras season in New Orleans.

Let's go see the Muses and the flambeaus
We'll follow that Zulu wherever he goes
Al Johnson, Fess, and big Earl King
We'll hear them whistle
and hear them sing
It's Mardi Gras season
in New Orleans.

Our first kiss was
at the crazy M.O.M.'s Ball
I was Sam Spade you were Lauren Bacall
You're so much fun when you're not you
Let's do it again for the Krewe du Vieux
It's Mardi Gras season in New Orleans.

We pass through this life, a little at a time
And when it's over, we don't have a dime
Just remember we're always young
Ask your self: What would be fun?
It's Mardi Gras season in New Orleans.

# At The Mardi Gras

*Vocals By Dyane Mitchell*

Come on you all
We're gonna have a ball
At the Mardi Gras
We'll be at Lee Circle
All dressed in purnurple
At the Mardi Gras

Now I got a friend
Down on Caffin Avenue
Who can give us a thrill
He's down at Puglia's

Rite on the side singing Blueberry Hill
We're having a party
Everybody's having fun
We're having a party

I got a godson,
He's got a shotgun
Rite on the route
He got barbecue
Wait for the krewe
And get ready to shout

# Prettiest Girl On Mardi Gras

*Vocals By Jerry Hess*

Some girls dream of a beach condo
Others want a playboy
with plenty of dough
Some even want to be a movie star
I just want to be the prettiest girl
on Mardi Gras

I'll wear some high heel shoes
and a bustier
To some it may be a little risqué
But I'll be the cutest thing
you ever saw
I want to be the prettiest girl
on Mardi Gras

CHORUS:
Now when I go out on Mardi Gras day
I'll have all the boys all looking my way
Even the King of Rex will be in awe
I want to be the prettiest girl
on Mardi Gras

I want to be the prettiest gal
on Mardi Gras
I want all the boys to say ooh la la
Give me rhinestones,
sequins and a convertible car
I want to be the prettiest girl
on Mardi Gras

# When The Levees Broke

*Vocals By Jerry Hess*

I had a dream about Mardi Gras
And a girl Katrina
Saw some floats floating away
When the levees broke
on Mardi Gras Day

Floating down the avenue
Saw coconuts and King Zulu
He was on a sacalait
When the levees broke
on Mardi Gras Day

CHORUS
When the levees broke
on Mardi Gras Day
When the levees broke
on Mardi Gras Day
From Holly Grove to Vieux Carre

When the levees broke
on Mardi Gras Day

Deacon John was on a baby grand
On a roof was the St. Aug Band
Ernie K-Doe was singing away
When the levees broke
on Mardi Gras Day

CHORUS

The dream was wild, man you know
I should be on top Touro
And then I woke on up
And there I was with a wet coconut

CHORUS

# The Prettiest "Girl" on Mardi Gras

## THE DEVIL AND MISTER JONES

*Photo by Author, Mardi Gras 1984, French Quarter*

# Appendix III

## New Orleans Recipes & Etchings
## By Robert Seago

# Red Beans and Rice

1lb. red beans
11/2 qts. water
1/2-1lb. seasoning meat, ham, or slab bacon
3 onions chopped

3 cloves garlic, chopped
1-2 bay leaves
2 tbsp. chopped celery/parsley
salt pepper to taste

Wash beans, cover with cold water and soak overnight. Place beans, onion, garlic, bay leaf, celery, and parsley in water. Cook until beans are beginning to soften. Add already cooked meat (usually boiled or fried) and continue cooking until beans are tender. Salt should be added when beans are nearly done to avoid toughening them. For a little extra zip add a few drops of tabasco sauce. Serve over rice with buttered French bread or rolls.

# Creole Filé Gumbo

1 cup each oil and flour
1 can each peeled tomatoes and tomato paste
1 cup each onion and celery, chopped
1 gallon water
1 lb. shrimp

1 lb. crabmeat or pieces of broken
crab
1/2 cup chopped bell pepper and
onion tops
bay leaf, garlic, salt, pepper,
filé seasoning

Heat oil in cast iron skillet. Add flour and cook stirring constantly to make
a dark roux. Add celery and onion to roux and saute. Add tomato paste and
some water. Allow to brown so mixture loses bright red coloring. Add peeled
tomatoes and simmer. Place shrimp, crab, bell pepper, onion tops, bay leaf, and
other seasonings in a large pot. Add water and skillet mixture, simmer 20 to
30 minutes. If gumbo is too thin add cornstarch dissolved in water to thicken.
Serve over rice and let each person add file to their own taste.

# Shrimp Creole

2 lbs. cleaned shrimp
3 tbsps. cooking oil or bacon fat
3 tbsps. flour
1 large onion
2 C. water
1 8oz. can tomato sauce
1 8oz. can tomatoes

1 clove & 1 pod garlic, minced
1/2 tsp thyme
1 bay leaf
2 tbsps. chopped green pepper
3 tbsps. chopped celery
dash of cayenne pepper
salt & pepper to taste

Saute onion in oil until tender (6-8 mins.) Stir in garlic & green pepper, and saute 2 mins. Blend in flour. Add tomatoes & sauce and simmer 5 mins. Stir in water, seasoning & shrimp. Cover & simmer 30 mins. Serve over rice.

# Oysters Rockefeller

1/2 lb. butter
1 large bunch spinach (fresh or frozen)
1 small bunch parsley
1 bunch green onions
2 tsp. worcestershire

2 or 3 dashes tabasco
4 tbls. catsup
1 oz. absinthe
bread crumbs
oyster shells and ice cream salt

Grind up spinach, parsley and onions fine. Drain off juice. Cook 10 mins. in pot with 1/2 lb. butter. Add worcestershire, tabasco and catsup. Cook 2-3 mins. Stirring . Add absinthe and then enough bread crumbs to thicken to pasty consistency. Wash shells with water only and place on ice cream salt. Place oysters in shell eye to eye. Put prepared mix on oysters in shell. Broil in oven under fire about 10 mins. with oven open. Watch closely. 1 dozen oysters.

# Bananas Foster

| | |
|---|---|
| 2 tbsp. brown sugar | dash of cinnamon |
| 1 tbsp. butter | 1/2 oz. banana liqueur |
| 1 ripe banana peeled and sliced | 1 oz. white rum |
| lengthwise | 1 large scoop vanilla ice cream |

Melt brown sugar and butter in flat chafing dish. Add banana and saute until tender (ripe banana.) Sprinkle with cinnamon. Pour in banana liqueur and rum over all. Light with match to flame. Baste with warm liquid until flame burns out. Serve immediately over ice cream. Serves 1 (one.)

# Praline

| | |
|---|---|
| 1 1/2 C. brown sugar | 2 C. pecans |
| 1 1/2 C. white sugar | 1/2 stick butter |
| 1 C. condensed milk | 1 pinch salt |

Mix together and cook until a cohesive ball forms in a glass of water. Add 1 tsp. vanilla & beat until it holds shape. Drop on wax paper & allow to cool. Recipe makes about 3 dozen pralines.

# Biographies

## About the Author

Maurice Le Gardeur was born and raised in New Orleans. He is a graduate of Jesuit High School and Tulane University, B.A. (1967) and J.D. (1972). For the last 37 years Maurice has resided on the Northshore of Lake Pontchartrain engaged in a "country law practice," primarily involving personal injury litigation. The father of three sons he resides with his wife, (and fellow lawyer) Meg Kern, and their six dogs and five cats at Hog Hollow, their 40 acre farm near Folsom, Louisiana. Maurice began writing poetry in 1982 and has become known as the *Bard of Boston Street*. From 1994-1997 he authored a weekly poetry column in the New Banner newspaper entitled *Ballards*. Maurice can be reached at www.bardofbostonstreet.com

## About the Artist

Robert Seago is a native of New Orleans who moved to the Northshore in 1984 where he maintains his art studio and musical pursuits. He still considers New Orleans his home "forever." He is married to Judy Hopkins, a retired St. Tammany Parish school teacher, and they have three children. Robert has many interests and pursues his love of the Big Bands with his own seventeen piece band, Seago's Sentimental Serenaders. Robert's love of art began in his younger years as he developed his skills in graphic arts, watercolor, oil and acrylic media. Mardi Gras scenes are a favorite subject, followed by landscapes and agricultural renderings. Robert displays his art in several art galleries in Florida and Louisiana. Many of his recent works can be viewed on his website at www.robertseagoart.com.

## About the Music

John Preble is the executive producer of the CD contained in this book (inside back cover pocket), and he is the owner and curator of the Abita Mystery House in Abita Springs, Louisiana. These New Orleans Carnival songs represent many genres of music—Pop, New Orleans Rhythm and Blues, Bluegrass, Novelty, Gospel, and Cajun. John wrote the music and lyrics to the New Orleans Mardi Gras Classics over a period of forty years. We hope you enjoy them. Additional copies can be ordered online at www.abitianrecords.com

# A Final Word for Texans

Like Blanche Dubois in *A Streetcar Named Desire*, New Orleans has always depended on the kindness of strangers, and Texans have always been our favorite strangers. The only Texan who is NOT welcome in New Orleans is W, who has given this letter of the alphabet a whole new meaning. In all fairness to Texas, although W was raised in Texas, he was born in New Haven, Connecticut and was a true Yankee in King Arthur's[1] Court.

So you folks from Texas come see us real soon—don't wait for Carnival and Mardi Gras because we might not survive the Summer. Look what Ike did to Galveston. Leave W and your Cadillacs at home and drive over in your King Ranch Edition F-150s with a full load of dirt for our levees. Drop it off at 7400 Leake[2] Avenue at the U.S. Army Corps of Engineers Headquarters in Carrollton—the highest ground in town.

While you're here eat lots of red beans and rice and andouille sausage po-boys (with whole-wheat Leidenheimer) at Mother's on Poydras or Luizza's on Bienville. On your way home please make a deposit[3] or two before you get north of Gramercy. KING-SIZED PORT-O-LETS (for Texans only) are located along Airline Highway between Zephyr Stadium and the Saints' Training Camp on David Drive to facilitate your delivery.[4] Honestly, I never thought I'd ever find myself asking Texans for a favor, but it's a small thing and not something you'd really miss.

It's a little known fact that Texas owes New Orleans a *Muchas Gracias* which W (who considers himself a student of histo-

---

1    A.K.A. Dick Cheney

2    I couldn't make this up if I wanted to, but how prescient—Leake Avenue predates the leaks in the U.S. Army Corps of Engineers' levee system protecting New Orleans.

3    New Orleans is constructed on alluvial soils deposited by the Mississippi River over the last 6,000 years, so your deposit won't be wasted.

4    WARNING! Don't use the smaller Pots O' Black & Gold on David Drive. Those are for the exclusive use of disgruntled Saints season ticket holders with chronic dysentery and playoff angst, and if they have been eating crawfish you DON'T want to go there!

ry) completely ignored. It's been suggested, by none other than a Texan,[5] that without the help and finances provided by some wealthy New Orleans businessmen and venture capitalists at Banks Arcade on Magazine Street, in support of the Texas Revolution, the State of Texas might still belong to Mexico, and the U.S. Border Patrol would be guarding the Sabine River, not the Rio Grande. Every tourist to San Antonio visits the Alamo, but how many Texans have been to the Banks Arcade site while in New Orleans?

In the final analysis it seems the JACKASSES may owe their very existence to the COONASSES!

*Au Revoir et Adios Amigos,*

# The Bard of B.S.

**Answer to Riddle of Carnival Mythology on page 40:**

Afrodite—the Goddess of Jazz

---

5    Edward L. Miller the author of *New Orleans and the Texas Revolution* (2004) published by the Texas A & M University Press.

# A Postscript to Carnival in New Orleans, a Fantasy

## And a Plea for your Financial Assistance

When Dorothy took off from that Kansas cornfield in Auntie Em's house she never dreamed she would land in Oz. When the people of New Orleans evacuated their beloved city, or were evacuated by the National Guard after Katrina, they never dreamed that some of them could never return to what to them is *Somewhere Over the Rainbow*—because to them the Land of Oz and New Orleans are one and the same.

When Dorothy wanted to go home all she had to do was close her eyes, click her ruby slippers together three times, and think to herself *there's no place like home* and magically she woke up back in Kansas with her family and friends around her. Our Displaced Dorothys (and there are thousands) don't have ruby slippers and, no matter how much they think there's no place like home, they can't come home because their houses are gone or collapsed in the Lower Nine; so they can't wake up from their nightmare of not being here in the Land of Dreams.

If you would like to help our Dorothys, their sisters and brothers return to Oz and the real-life Emerald City of New Orleans please send your tax free contributions to the Make it Right Foundation at:

Make It Right
P.O. Box 58009
New Orleans, La 70158
www.makeitrightnola.org

Remember, there's no place like home especially if your home is New Orleans. The people of New Orleans thank you for your generosity. *Merci Beaucoup!*

# Carne Vale Tuesday, Ashes Wednesday!

## SISTER'S NAUGHTY HABIT

*Photo by Author, Mardi Gras 1984, French Quarter*

# Pax Vobiscum.

# Sweet Dreams

Some find comfort
In the middle of the night
That things won't change
Although the weather might.